ELISSA THOMPSON

DRAWING
CALIFORNIA'S
SIGHTS AND SYMBOLS

E | Enslow Publishing
101 W. 23rd Street
Suite 240
New York, NY 10011
USA
enslow.com

Published in 2019 by Enslow Publishing, LLC.
101 W. 23rd Street, Suite 240, New York, NY 10011

Library of Congress Cataloging-in-Publication Data
Names: Thompson, Elissa, author.
Title: Drawing California's sights and symbols / Elissa Thompson.
Description: New York : Enslow Publishing, 2019. | Series: Drawing our states | Includes bibliographical references and index.
Audience: Grades 2-5.
Identifiers: LCCN 2018006915| ISBN 9781978503144 (library bound) | ISBN 9781978503120 (pbk.) | ISBN 9781978503137 (6 pack)
Subjects: LCSH: California—In art—Juvenile literature. | Emblems in art—Juvenile literature. | Drawing—Technique—Juvenile literature.
Classification: LCC NC825.C35 T49 2018 | DDC 741.2—dc23
LC record available at https://lccn.loc.gov/2018006915

Printed in the United States of America

To Our Readers: We have done our best to make sure all websites in this book were active and appropriate when we went to press. However, the author and the publisher have no control over and assume no liability for the material available on those websites or on any websites they may link to. Any comments or suggestions can be sent by email to customerservice@enslow.com.

Photo Credits: Cover and p.1 inset illustration and interior pages instructional illustrations by Laura Murawski.

Cover, p. 1 atsurkan/Shutterstock.com; p. 6 Michael Warwick/Shutterstock.com; p. 9 © The Feitelson / Lundeberg Art Foundation, courtesy Louis Stern Fine Arts Arts; p. 10 Creative Jen Designs/Shutterstock.com; p. 12 Alexander Zavadsky/Shutterstock.com; p. 14 Lukasz Stefanski/Shutterstock.com; p. 16 Try Media/ Shutterstock.com; p. 18 Valentyna Chukhlyebova/Shutterstock.com; p. 20 Tinnaporn Sathapornnanont/Shutterstock.com; p. 22 Mikhail Pogosov/ Shutterstock.com; p. 24 George Lepp/Photographer's Choice/Getty Images; p. 26 FiledImage/Shutterstock.com; p. 28 SchnepfDesign/Shutterstock.com.

CONTENTS

Words to Know   4

Welcome to California!   5

Meet Helen Lundenburg   8

Miles of Coastline: Map of California   10

31 Stars for States: The Great Seal of California   12

The California Bear Flag: A Grizzly and a Star   14

State Wildflower: California Golden Poppy   16

Smilodon! Saber-Toothed Tiger   18

Red-Cabled Landmark: The Golden Gate Bridge   20

Spanish History: A California Mission   22

Flocking Fun: The California Quail   24

Tallest in the World: The California Redwood Tree   26

Sacramento's Pride: California's Capital   28

Facts About California   30

Learn More   31

Index   32

WORDS TO KNOW

Cenozoic A time period more than sixty-five million years ago.

colonize To settle in a new land and claim it for the government of another country.

convert To change from one religious belief to another.

extinct No longer existing.

mining Removing minerals, like gold, from the ground.

navigator An explorer of the seas.

republic A form of government in which the authority belongs to the people.

rotunda A round dome.

saber-toothed Having a long, sharp tooth.

tribute An act of generosity toward a person.

WELCOME TO CALIFORNIA!

The state of California is home to many important businesses and jobs. These industries are so successful that if California were its own country, it would rank sixth in the world for the amount of money it makes!

California's wealth started with its agriculture. Its major cash products are cattle, milk, almonds, and grapes. The state produces about one-third of the nation's vegetables and two-thirds of the United States' fruits and nuts. California is proud of its wines. Eighty-five percent of all the wine made in the United States is produced in California.

Much of the world's movie and entertainment industry is located in Los Angeles, California. California also has an important computer industry. Silicon Valley stretches for about 25 miles (40 kilometers) in west-central California.

California is the third-largest state in the United States. It covers more than 150,000 square miles (400,000 sq. km). On September 9, 1850, California was the thirty-first state to join the nation. More than thirty-nine million people live in California, more than in any other state. Los Angeles and San Diego are the state's two most populated

Napa Valley in Northern California is known for its beautiful hills, productive wineries, and delicious food.

cities. The state capital is Sacramento. The Pacific Ocean runs along California's west coast. Mount Whitney, the highest mountain in the contiguous United States, is in California, and the lowest point, Death Valley, is also in California.

In September 1542, a Portuguese navigator named Juan Rodriguez Cabrillo was the first European to set foot in what is now California. It wasn't until 1848, when John Sutter struck gold in California, that foreigners from all over came to the state.

California is often called the Golden State because of the discovery of this precious metal.

This book will show you how to draw some of California's exciting sights and symbols. All the drawings begin with a simple shape. Under every drawing, directions explain how to do the step. Each new step is shown in red. The last step of most of the drawings is to add shading— just tilt your pencil to the side and hold it with your index finger. The more you draw, the better you will get at it. Good luck and have fun!

You will need the following supplies to draw California's sights and symbols:

- A sketch pad
- An eraser

- A number 2 pencil
- A pencil sharpener

These are some of the shapes and drawing terms you need to know to draw California's sights and symbols:

- Shading
- Squiggle
- Teardrop
- Vertical line
- Wavy line

- 3-D box
- Almond shape
- Horizontal line
- Oval
- Rectangle

MEET HELEN LUNDENBURG

Californian and artist Helen Lundenburg created the New Classicism, or Post Surrealism, art movement with her husband, Lorser Feitelson. New Classicism was a combination of dream-like images and structure and began in California in the 1930s and 1940s.

Born in Illinois, Lundenburg moved to Pasadena, California, as a child. At first she planned to be a writer. But then she met her husband, who convinced her to use her talents to become a painter. Helen loved the outdoors and painted many landscapes—though she did it from memory. She did not like to work outside—because one time she tried it and the wind blew her things away!

During the Great Depression, it was difficult for many people to find jobs. To make money during this time, Lundenburg painted several murals, or large paintings, for the government as part of a program to help those in need find work. These large pieces, painted on buildings, included one at the City Hall in Fullerton, California, called *The History of California*. The mural told the story of California, including the

Lundenburg's *Two Mountains* shows the
pastels she used in her work later in her career.

Spanish explorers arriving in the state and the growth of glamorous
Hollywood.

As her career continued, Lundenburg worked in softer, lighter colors,
creating calming landscapes, like this painting, *Two Mountains*. The
reflection of the mountain in the lake below makes you think about
what is real and what is not. Helen painted *Two Mountains* when she
was eighty-two years old. She died in 1999, at the age of ninety-one.

Miles of Coastline: Map of California

California has three states as neighbors: Nevada, Arizona, and Oregon—it also borders a country: Mexico! California has twelve regions, or

areas: the Sierra Nevada mountain range and four famous national parks, Death Valley National Park, Yosemite National Park, Sequoia National Park, and Kings Canyon National Park. Inyo National Forest has bristlecone pine trees that are 4,700 years old — the oldest living things on Earth!

- The North Coast
- San Francisco and the Bay Area
- Central Valley
- Central Coast
- Los Angeles County
- Orange County
- San Diego County
- Shasta Cascade
- Gold County
- The Deserts
- The High Sierras
- The Inland Empire

1

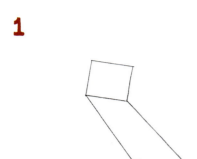

Draw a square and draw the angled shape as shown. Add some angled lines as shown.

2

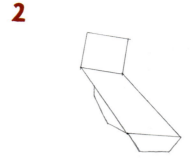

Soften or curve the angled lines.

3

You just drew the state of California! Now let's draw some of California's important places.

4

Draw a star for the capital, Sacramento. Draw the V shapes as shown for Death Valley.

5

Draw a dot for Mission San Luis Rey de Francia. Draw a curvy line for the Sacramento River.

6

Draw a square with a triangle on the top of it for Yosemite National Park. Draw two circles and a half-moon for Disneyland.

31 Stars for States: The Great Seal of California

Designed by US Army major R. S. Garnett, the California state seal has thirty-one stars at the top. The stars are for each state in the Union when California became a state in 1850. Under the stars is an ancient Greek word, *eureka*. It means "I found it" and is a tribute to the California's gold rush miners. Near the center is Minerva, Roman goddess of wisdom, and a grizzly bear, California's state animal. A man mines in the Sacramento River with ships behind him as the Sierra Nevada mountains stand tall in the background.

1

To draw one of the ships featured in the seal, begin with an angled shape. This is the overall basic shape of the boat.

2

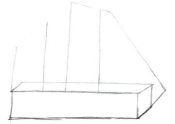

At the bottom of the shape, draw a 3-D rectangle box. Draw three vertical lines that extend from the rectangle up to the top of the shape. These are guides for the sails.

3

Draw a curved line on the right side of the rectangle. Add horizontal lines over the vertical lines. These lines are for the sails.

4

Continue drawing the sails as shown. Draw a pointy shape on the left side. This is the back sail.

5

Draw a triangle. Connect it to a curved, rectangular shape on the lower right. Draw curved lines on the rectangle.

6

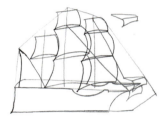

Draw a triangle on the left side. Draw little rectangles on the bottom for windows. Draw horizontal lines on the bottom.

7

Draw lines on the sails to show that the wind is blowing. Shade in the middle of the bottom rectangle to complete your ship.

8

Draw three circles. The smallest circle is the head and the larger circles are the body.

The California Bear Flag: A Grizzly and a Star

The California Bear Flag has a white background with a grizzly bear above the words "California Republic." It became the state flag in 1911. In the early 1800s, California had nearly ten thousand grizzly bears. Today there are none! As people moved to California, they killed the grizzlies for their skins and food. A red star sits at the top left corner of the flag, a copy of the lone star of Texas, and there is a red border on the bottom.

1

Draw three circles. The smallest circle is the head and the larger circles are the body.

2

Draw upside-down triangles underneath the circles. These are the legs. Notice how some of the lines are curved and some are straight.

3

Connect all of these shapes together by drawing curved lines between the circles, shaping the body and neck. Square off the tips of the triangles to make the feet of the bear. For the mouth, draw a little rectangle on the head circle.

4

To finish the head, draw a small triangle in the rectangle for the mouth. Draw another triangle for the ear. Draw a five-pointed star as shown.

5

Draw the shape underneath the bear. Draw the border on the bottom. Write the words "California Republic" above the border. The last step is to either shade in the star and the border or color them in with a red pencil.

State Wildflower: California Golden Poppy

The California golden poppy (*Eschscholtzia californica*) became California's state flower on March 2, 1903. The golden poppy is a

wildflower that grows all over California. French author and naturalist Adelbert von Chamisso first wrote about this flower in 1816. When his ship landed in San Francisco in October 1816, these poppies were among the few plants still in bloom. Native Americans used poppies for food and in medicines.

2

1

Begin by drawing a curved, upside-down triangular shape. This is the bulb.

On the bottom of the bulb, draw a small rectangle. Then draw another smaller, upside-down triangle. Extend the point of the triangle until you have a straight line coming down the page.

3

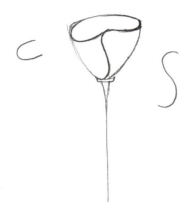

4

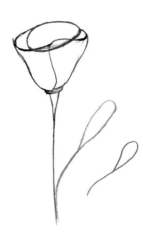

Draw a skinny S in the middle of the bulb. Extend and curve the top of the S toward the right. Draw a C shape on the other side of the flower. These are the outer petals.

On top of the bud, draw an egg shape that's turned on its side. This is the inner petal. Draw a line that extends from the stem on the lower right and loop it back, making a paddle-like shape. This is the bud.

5

6

Erase where the egg shape overlaps the front petals. Draw a wavy line in the bud. Add a diagonal line underneath the wavy line in the bud. Add the leaves by drawing lines that extend out from the stem. Draw the lines on either side of the stem.

Shade in the areas as shown using the tip of your pencil and very lightly, line by line, shade in the areas. Add lines to the leaves to finish.

Smilodon! Saber-Toothed Tiger

The saber-toothed tiger *Smilodon* is California's state fossil. Saber-toothed tigers lived in the Cenozoic era, more than sixty-five million years ago. The *Smilodon* is not really a tiger but a mammal ancestor of cats, dogs, bears, and weasels. It is called a tiger because that is the animal it most looks like today. The *Smilodon* became extinct about ten thousand years ago. Thousands of *Smilodon* fossils have been found in the La Brea Tar Pits since 1912. Today you can visit the tar pits in Los Angeles.

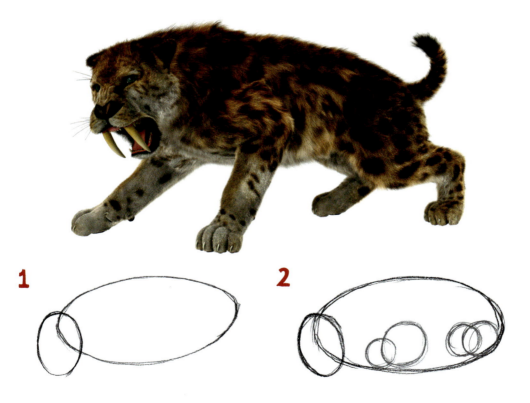

1

2

Begin by drawing a long, skinny oval. This is the body. Draw another, smaller oval to the left. This is the head.

Draw four circles on top of the larger oval. These will guide you when drawing the legs, in the next step.

3

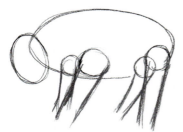

Adding on to those circles, draw lines extending down. These are the legs.

4

Finish the legs by connecting the lines with C shapes. Using the lines as guides, curve them to shape the legs. Draw the neck by making more curved lines as shown.

5

Draw pointy, triangular shapes as shown. These are the ears and tail. Draw a curved line for the mouth, which is open wide. Add curved lines on the belly. Erase any extra lines.

6

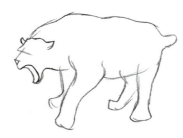

Draw a T in the middle of the face. This will guide you to draw the nose and the eyes. Draw an upside-down triangle for the nose. Draw a curved shape for the mouth.

7

Draw in the eye as shown. Add claws to the feet. Erase extra lines.

Red-Cabled Landmark: The Golden Gate Bridge

The Golden Gate Bridge in California stretches 1.7 miles (2.7 km) from San Francisco to Marin County. After four years of work, the Golden Gate Bridge was finished in 1937. It was designed by Joseph Strauss, a Chicago engineer, and cost about $35 million to build. The bridge has six lanes and is 260 feet (79 meters) above the San Francisco Bay. People from all over the world come to see this famous landmark. Every day, 120,000 cars, buses, and trucks drive across the bridge!

1

Begin by drawing a horizontal line. Divide that line with three vertical lines. Notice where those vertical lines are placed.

2

Draw another horizontal line above the first horizontal line, as a guide. Draw two triangles as shown.

3

Curve the lines in the triangles in the center of the bridge. Draw in two thin shapes as shown. These are the supports. Notice how those shapes are in the center of the triangles. Draw in a wavy line underneath those shapes to show the ocean.

4

Add another line underneath the bridge. Shade in those tall, thin shapes. Draw straight vertical lines as shown. These are the cables.

Spanish History: A California Mission

Missions are places where religious leaders teach others about a religion. Spanish settlers wanted to colonize California, so they built missions throughout the state. The Spanish hoped to convert the Native Americans to Christianity and have them be part of the Spanish Empire. Between July 16, 1769, and July 4, 1823, the Spanish built twenty-one missions in California. Fray Lasuén founded Mission San Luis Rey de Francia in 1798. It is the largest of the twenty-one missions built along the coast of California.

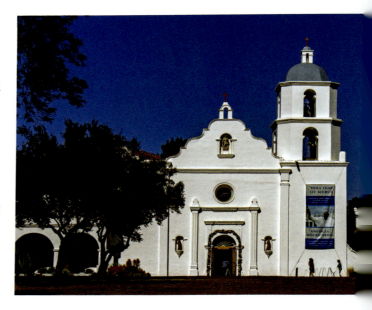

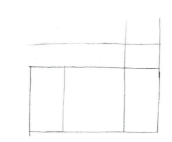

2

Divide the rectangle into three sections by drawing two vertical lines. The first and third sections should be the same size. Extend the lines on the right rectangle up. Draw a horizontal line that crosses the vertical lines.

1

To draw Mission San Luis Rey de Francia, begin by drawing a rectangle.

3

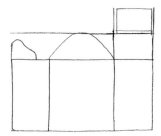

Draw a triangle above the middle rectangle. Draw a curved shape above the left rectangle. Draw a smaller rectangle within the rectangle on the upper right. Excellent!

4

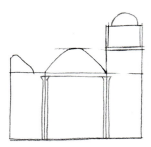

Now add a semicircle on top. Draw a line across the top of the middle box. Add two lines down on either side for columns.

5

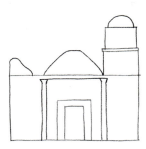

Erase the lines in the columns and in the top right rectangle. Draw a rectangle within a rectangle in the middle rectangle.

6

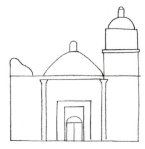

Draw in the door as shown. Draw two upside-down U shapes on top as shown.

7

Draw more upside-down U shapes as shown. Draw the circle on top of the door.

8

Draw the crosses. Add the vertical lines and the shape on top of the left rectangle.

Flocking Fun: The California Quail

In 1931, California chose the quail as its state bird. The California quail is a small, round bird about 8 inches (20 centimeters) long. Quails have funny-looking feathers rising off the tops of their heads, called a nodding crest. The quail's head is usually black with white stripes. Though both the male and female quails' bodies are gray, brown, and white, the male has many more black-and-white markings. Although quails can fly, they are usually seen walking or running on the ground.

1

Begin by drawing an oval. This is the body.

2

Draw a circle to the upper left. This is the head.

3

Connect the circle and the oval with curved lines. Draw a curvy triangle at the bottom of the oval. This is the body.

4

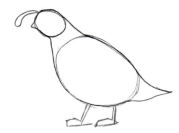

Draw the curvy shape on top of the head. This is the nodding crest. For the beak, draw a little bump on the side of the head. Now, draw in the legs underneath the body as shown.

5

Draw a little circle for the eye. Draw a line in the beak. Extend the line onto the head and neck. This is a guide for shading in the next step. Lightly draw in the wings as shown.

6

Shade in the drawing slowly and lightly, using the side of your pencil. Use the lines in the head, neck, body, and wings as guides.

Tallest in the World: The California Redwood Tree

California redwood trees are amazing giants. They can live for more than two thousand years! The redwood became the state's official tree in 1937. There are two types of California redwoods: the coast redwood and the giant sequoia. At Redwood National Park, you can find a coast redwood that is 368 feet (112 m) tall. This is the world's tallest tree. At Sequoia National Park, there is a giant sequoia tree that weighs 6,000 tons (5,443 metric tons) and is 36 feet (11 m) wide! This is the largest tree in the world.

GENERAL SHERMAN

1

Draw a tall, thin triangle. This is the trunk.

2

Turn your pencil on its side and lightly shade from side to side on top of the trunk. Practice shading this way on a piece of scrap paper. Hold the pencil lightly while you stroke the paper gently. Well done! You have drawn the area of the branches and leaves.

3

Darken the shaded areas as shown. These are the branches and leaves.

4

Adding to the branches and leaves, draw straight and curved lines throughout the tree to add detail to the branches.

5

Finally, shade in the trunk, turning your pencil on its side again. Shade the trunk by sweeping your pencil up and down the tall trunk.

Sacramento's Pride: California's Capital

Sacramento, California's capital, is home to the California State Capitol Building. Designed in 1860 by Miner F. Butler and Rueben Clark, it took almost fifteen years to build and cost $2.4 million. The architectural style of the building is the Renaissance revival style. The building is 220 feet (67 m) tall. The front of the building has eight freestanding columns. The Capitol has a beautiful dome, or rotunda. The governor of California works in the building with many other government officials.

1

2

Begin by drawing a long rectangle. This is the base of the Capitol.

Divide the rectangle equally into three sections by drawing two vertical lines.

3

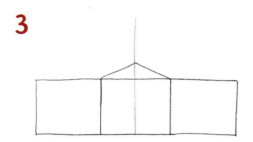

First draw a light vertical line in the middle of the center rectangle. Using this line as a guide, draw a triangle above the middle rectangle as shown.

4

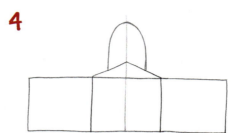

Add an upside-down U shape on top of the triangle. This is the dome.

5

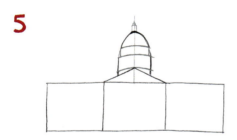

Draw curved lines in the upside-down U shape. Add a mini dome shape on top.

6

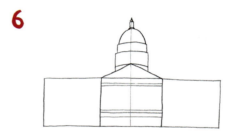

Going back to the middle rectangle, draw five horizontal lines as shown.

7

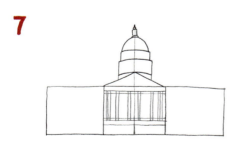

Using those horizontal lines as guides, draw vertical lines. These are the columns.

8

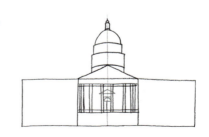

Finish with the shapes as shown.

FACTS ABOUT CALIFORNIA

Statehood • September 9, 1850, 31st state
Area • 158,869 square miles (411,469 sq. km)
State Population • 39,536,653
Capital • Sacramento, population, 493,025
Most Populated City • Los Angeles, population, 4,041,707
Industries • Film, electronics, computers, software, petroleum,
    tourism, wine
Agriculture • Vegetables, fruit, grapes, dairy products
Animal • California grizzly bear
Dance • West Coast swing dance
Bird • California quail
Flower • California golden poppy
Fish • Golden trout
Fossil • Saber-toothed tiger
Tree • California redwood
Gemstone • Benitote
Insect • California Dogface butterfly
Marine Animal • California gray whale
Mineral • Native gold
Reptile • California desert tortoise
Rock • Serpentine
Nickname • The Golden State

LEARN MORE

Books

Mihaly, Christy. *Natural Wonders of the World: California's Redwood Forest*. Mendota Heights, MN: Focus Readers, 2018.

Newman, Lauren. *California*. New York, NY: Scholastic, 2018.

Raum, Elizabeth. *The California Gold Rush: An Interactive History Adventure*. North Mankato, MN: Capstone Press, 2016.

Wilson, Steve. *The California Gold Rush: Chinese Laborers in America*. New York, NY: Rosen Publishing Group, 2016.

Websites

Kids Connect with California Agriculture

https://www.cdfa.ca.gov/Kids/

Learn all about the livestock and crops that come from California. Take a quiz on avocados or play food detective.

Oakland Museum of California: California's Untold Stories: Gold Rush!

http://explore.museumca.org/goldrush

Experience the California gold rush with this interactive website. You can even tour an exhibit in the museum.

INDEX

A

agriculture, 5

C

Cabrillo, Juan Rodriguez, 6
California golden poppy, 16–17
California quail, 24–25
California redwood tree, 26–27
capital, 28–29
Cenozoic era, 18
Chamisso, Adelbert von, 16

D

Death Valley, 6, 10–11

G

Golden Gate Bridge, 20–21
great seal, 12–13
grizzly bear, 12, 14–15

L

La Brea Tar Pits, 18–19
Los Angeles, 5, 10, 18
Lundenburg, Helen, 8–9

M

map, 10–11
Mission San Luis Rey de Francia, 11, 22–23
Mount Whitney, 6

P

Pacific Ocean, 6

R

Renaissance revival, 28

S

saber-toothed tiger, 18–19
Sacramento, 6, 11–12, 28
Sequoia National Park, 10, 26–27
Silicon Valley, 5
state flag, 14–15

T

Two Mountains, 9